Fashion Style Guide

10 Tricks For the Perfect Outfit for Every Occasion That Leverage Your Natural Beauty

By Joanne Robinson

Table of Contents

Introduction

When it comes to the fashion world, the rules are meant to be broken. In fact, rule breaking is the process that gives rise to a new fashion trend, which makes it more challenging to find the perfect outfit for different occasions. With a myriad of varieties, fabrics, and colors to choose from, making the final choice may feel like a daunting task to complete.

Your outfit for a given occasion sets up your individuality as well as personality. The outfit can make you a shining star of an occasion, and can also turn you into just another dressed up person; it all comes down to the final selection of your outfit. People perceive their outfit as part of what and who they are. If you do not have an as good fashion sense as a fashion expert then it's not the reason to be concerned about; with the right kind of insights and outfit knowledge, you can be master of making your own choices for the perfect outfit.

Make no mistake. Whether you feel good about it or not, but people start making opinions about you based on the outfit. If you wish to stand out from the crowd and make a stunning impression, the time is right to get yourself familiarized with the art of selecting the best outfit for a given occasion.

The Science of Color

Each person carries its unique personality traits and physical attributes. That is why your must realize what color does the justice to your attributes including eye coloring, hair, skin tone, etc. For instance, if you have olive-colored or brown skin with darker eyes and hair; jewel-tones outfits suits the best and brings out your real charming personality. Similarly, popular choices for party dresses for female are rich purples, pinks, deep, and golds.

Taking another example, if your skin tone is beige-colored or ivory then the ideal choice is the one that can optimally brings out your skin undertone. An outfit with a real or royal blue shade beautifully accents bluish undertones. Similarly, red or pink toned skin matches beautifully with peach colored outfits.

The Choice of Fabric

You might come across outfits matching ideally with your skin tone; however, before making the final choice, the quality of the fabric should be taken into consideration. Saving few bucks and pick an outfit made from a low-quality fabric is not going to do the trick. Always spend the extra bucks to get hold of quality outfit that can reflect your true persona. Outfits made from quality materials also create minimal discomfort in problem areas and give you a comfortable experience.

In the end, the goal should be of making your outfit finalizing experience exciting and not a stressful one. Following chapters of the book highlights the best outfit choices for different occasions such as a first date, business party, cocktail party, and so on. Fall in love with your outfit and look your best!

Chapter 1: Be a Start at a Wedding Function

Let the hour, the season, and the invitation be your best companions to pick the final dress for the upcoming wedding ceremony.

For Eves

Red and black outfits are all time favorite and charming. If you feel that the final selection is really becoming hard, then you can also consult with the bride, bride's mother, or maid of honor. Taking advice from the right person can greatly assist in resolving the outfit dilemma.

If the wedding ceremony is scheduled for daytime, then heavily beaded dresses should be avoided as day weddings are expected to be more casual. One can consider wearing knee-length outfits made from cotton, especially in warmer regions or weather; also for weddings taking place in warmer weather or regions, such outfits also goes nicely with open-toed shoes or simple hats.

In case, the ceremony and reception are scheduled for afternoon and evening respectively, and the invitation is unclear about the dress type, then usually, the wedding is going to be a semi-formal affair. Such ceremonies call for evening suits or cocktail dresses; however, ensure that your outfit color is not upstaging the bride. For instance, rather than going for a hot pink, wear pale pink outfit.

Except for the grandest ceremonies, outfits as short as knee-lengths are welcoming, given that they have a formal or semi-formal fabric and cut. For instance, a silk blend or pure silk is an appropriate choice. If you have decided to wear a sleeveless or strapless outfit in a house of worship and the wedding environment is strict about covering up, then ensure that you are carrying a wrap along with you.

Also, if you are also going to attend the rehearsal dinner, then you must note that it varies greatly in terms of formality. In most rehearsal dinners, cocktail-party rules apply. Save your precious outfit for the big wedding day; for the dinner, you can go with a dress and a cardigan or jacket with some added sparkles.

For Adams

Modern men are known for not being afraid to embrace fashion. It's your natural desire to look timeless, sophisticated, and stylish for the upcoming wedding ceremony. Black is one of the popular choices but there is a myriad of other options as well. Brown, navy, gray and even brighter shades are also great ones to pick from. Final selection of your outfit depends on your personal taste, wedding theme, and style.

Research Fabrics

It's not all about colors and the style of your suite. Also, ensure that you have selected the suit made from the right kind of fabric. The right kind of fabric ensures ideal comfort to keep you at your best on the big day.

Consult with your tailor or groomsmen about different kinds of styles and fabrics to go with. For instance, if you are attending a summer wedding then a velvet suit is not the ideal type as it is too warm for the summer season and also looks clingy.

Chapter 2: Pick a Classy Outfit for a Company/Business Party

Your strong craving to dress up perfectly for a business/company party is justifiable; after all, who doesn't like to dress at his/her best and indulge in a quality interaction with other business professionals. One of the most popular choices for such a professional occasion is to wear something stylish and comforting.

It may not be a bad idea to interact with the host prior to the party. Many times, a host has set up a unique business theme and people come to the party without being aware of the theme. Even if there is no particular theme, have a quick chat with the host to get some useful advice and information about the event.

Maintain the Professional Feel

Be it any type of business/company party, it calls for maintaining a certain level of maturity with respect to outfit selection. For instance, funky colors and shades reflecting your enthusiasm to plan a summer holiday trip is probably not the best choice for the occasion. However, that doesn't mean that one cannot pick a fun outfit; a fun outfit with a professional touch perfectly fits in. Just ensure that your outfit is not stripping away your mature look.

For Adams

Of course, you want to create an instant impact on the onlookers in your upcoming party with the right outfit choice. For men, custom tailored suits are quite famous as they look incredible on a manly physique. One great thing about custom suits is that one can add numerous special touches such as a unique monogram. Your desired special touch assists you in revealing your true identity.

Another popular choice is wearing a polo or buttoned-down shirt along with dress pants or khakis. One can also layer the outfit with a blazer, v-neck sweater, or a sport coat to give it a complete look. You can also wear a tie with it, but it's always optional.

Select an Outfit Matching Your Complexion

Matching of the final outfit with your color and look is quite important. If your look is dusky, pick the one that enhances your dusky appeal. Avoid outfits with too much designing and patterns as they are considered inappropriate for formal occasions and parties.

For Eves

Looking graceful and gorgeous for office lunch/dinner parties is not just a requirement but it's more like a compulsion for women. The outfit you are looking for is the one that can flatter you figure. Custom tailored individual style outfit is one of the popular choices for such occasions. Custom tailored outfit allows you to design it to perfectly fit your unique figure. The key is to keep things professional while being in line with the professional event.

Pick Your Ideal Wear

Dress pants, khakis, or a skirt paired with three-quarter or long sleeve tops is one ideal choice. If you are planning to wear gowns or skirts then ensure that you have selected an outfit made from high-quality fabric. For summer or spring parties, bold colors are also great ones to pick. For fall parties, outfits with red, blue or golden shades are quite suitable. Also, for fall parties, make sure that the fabric of your outfit is easily movable with your body.

Irrespective of the occasion or office environment, try avoiding outfits that are provocative. Your choice of outfit may adversely impact your career instead of helping.
Too much revealing outfits might jeopardize your chances of being promoted.

Trousers along with a blouse and blazer or refined sweater are also an appropriate choice as they give you a quite professional touch. In case you have to attend the party right after you leave the office, then a wrap dress or sheath with darker tone is a good choice. Also, you can try a suit and a feminine blouse along with appropriate shoes.

Chapter 3: Look Elegant at a Dinner Party

Selecting the perfect outfit for a dinner party involves a lot of gray areas. It's not only about looking good as people are more concerned about not overdoing it.

For Eves

For a dinner party, one can never go out of fashion with a gorgeous black outfit. It spares you from wondering whether you are dressy enough or not. A simple yet stunning black dress is a sophisticated enough choice which does not give the feel of being overly dressed. Paired your black dress with a stylish red shoe and you will have a fail-safe holiday attire which will suit all kinds of dinner parties.

What's the Ideal Choice?

Practically there is no ideal choice as an ideal dinner party wear varies based on the host, dinner occasion as well as time of year; that makes the choice a little tricky. For instance, if you are underdressed for the occasion then it might offend other dinner companions. On the other side, if you are too much overdressed then you might end up making dinner companions uncomfortable, inadequate and even insecure. The best way to be safe is to discuss with the host as it will tell you whether the dinner party is a skirt and blouse, buttoned-up affair or a denim get-to-gather type affair.

In case you are in a dilemma until the last moment, then it's always safe to carry a lovely scarf and dangly earrings, in case the party calls for more dressing up.

For Adams

Most fashion experts suggest avoiding buttoned-down shirts in white shades along with neckties. Instead, one can go with a dark or neutral shaded shirt; a sweater on top also goes well with the shirt, but it's optional.

For evening dinner parties, dress slacks or khakis is also an ideal choice. If you feel that the party is of casual type, then khaki pants made from cotton goes nicely with the casual tone. Also, if the party is going to last for hours, then you can opt for jeans; dark, indigo-shaded jeans will give a new and crisp look. Pick your footwear that fits in perfectly with your dark shaded jeans.

Warm-weather Dinner Party

For warm weather parties, you can go with a buttoned-down shirt with short sleeves. A pressed, crisp pair of walking shorts also suits for outdoor dinner parties. For evening parties, khaki-styled pants or jeans are one of the popular choices and suits perfectly with the occasion.

Chapter 4: Be a Knockout at a Cocktail Party

So your invitation for the dream cocktail party has arrived and yet you are in a dilemma about what to wear. Standing out in grand affairs such as a cocktail party can be quite challenging. Be it men or women, everyone wishes to get hands on the perfect attire that can make him/her a knockout at a cocktail party.

For Eves

Shorter outfits with frill are quite famous for such a special event. Also, the classic short black dress can make you a hit at the party; the black dress is the outfit that can reflect your personality by accessorizing your mood. Specially made cocktail dresses are always a great choice; however, there are other options as well.

What Suits the Best?

Irrespective of modern trends, pick your ideal cocktail outfit based on a color, cut and style that can complement with your skin tone and curves. A-line styles, as well as empire waists, perfectly complement most body shapes. Also stylish ball-gown cuts are not a bad choice to go with.

A modern cocktail party can be a casual get-to-gather affair with a platter crudités, and it can also be a swanky society affair. However, most cocktail parties call for more of dressy-casual attire; a stunning top with some added special details along with a tailored pants or skirt, plus fancy flats or heels perfectly suit the occasion. Fashion experts suggest avoiding too casual fabrics such as denim, jersey, and chino.

Another great choice is wearing a fine-gauge merino wool top or cashmere along with a satin skirt (knee-length); give the outfit a classy touch with stacked bangles for arms and matching heels. You can also consider wearing a pantsuit if it's not too corporate. However, as you know that different cities have their unique dress codes, you must make a choice based on the local code; a cocktail dress that can also be perceived as too dressy in one region and too casual in other.

For Adams

Most cocktail parties are casual, relaxed affairs which demand stylish dressing to stun the crowd. For daytime or afternoon cocktail parties, you have the liberty to add more patterns and colors to the outfit. The key to nail the cocktail dress code is to create a fine balance between youthful silhouette and traditional aesthetic.

One can go with a fine combination of a coat, dark suit, and tie. Also for some cocktail parties, you can also opt for a stylish jacket and tie paired with dark jeans; however, the choice should be made based on how casual the party environment is.

Blazers and Suits

To compliment the cocktail look, pick a stunningly designed semi-formal blazers and trousers or custom tailored suit. For cocktail attires, darker suits are among traditional choices, so keep things classy by opting for muted grays, subdued cobalt, or dusky navies. Tailored suits are great, but ensure that they are not too tight. Also, ensure that your blazer figure is modern, fresh, and hugging. In order to perfectly fit into the night as well as transitional day looks, ensure that your outfit is adaptable with basic suits. You can style up your attire with inventive accessories and pocket squares to give yourself the perfect classic touch.

Shirts

Give yourself a cool makeover for your cocktail party with fitted dress shirts. Powder blue or white shaded shirts are safe to wear and give classic touch. A bright and modern styled button down shirt delivers a stunning edge to your cocktail outfit; however, ensure that they are not too much over your top.

Chapter 5: Dress Up Perfectly for a Job Interview

The first 5-10 seconds after you walk in the interview room make your first impression to a fellow denizen or an interviewer. Many times, it's quite difficult to undone the damage created by your improper outfit.

Your outfit for the interview can give you a free pass to its next level. Take full advantage of your outfit, and add the perfect look to your corporate experience and skills set.

Understand the Company's Dress Code
Apart from learning the work setting of your dream company, priorities on knowing about its particular dress code, prior to your interview. Many times, a company seems to have a semi-open infrastructure, but it might be having strict office dress code. If you get a chance to meet one of the company's employees, then he/she can guide you through their dress code and more.

For Eves

Suits are very common and acceptable interview attire; however, you can explore many other choices.

Give Yourself the Best Interview Look

If a company prefers traditional interview outfit, then you can't go wrong with a professional suit. Even with a suit, you can explore varieties with a range of available designs. Technological advancements in retail and media sectors have made way for out of box suites that provide modern touch along with maintaining professionalism.

Many companies don't mind skirts or slacks with or without blazers on top. However, wearing a hose is mandatory with skirts as bare legs are not acceptable, even for long skirts. A pencil skirt along with a stylish blouse or a sheath dress with a cardigan and wide belt also blends in perfectly with an interview environment; it also reflects your personal sense of style. Apart from classical black, you can go with a brown or navy shaded attire. Also, you can wear lighter plain shades, especially in the summer. No matter how casual a company environment is, it is never appropriate to go with jeans.

Many people make a mistake by assuming that the job is theirs and then end up wearing something unacceptable; it's also not a bad idea to contact the interview assistant for suggestions. Ensure that your outfit is perfectly tailored, clean and ironed. After all the hard work you have done in selecting the perfect attire, you don't want to wear something tight, plunging or skimpy.

For Adams

Give yourself an added advantage by dressing one level higher than the standard, everyday office attire. If the company environment is more casual, then it's always safe to wear business casual.

Your Interview Suit

Suits are common wear that suit perfectly for different corporate environments. For selecting your favorite interview suit, the focus should be on fabric, style and its fitting. If you are opting for a readymade suit then ensure that it is not too big or boxy for your body type. If you want to avoid any fitting issues then go for a tailored suit that makes you look busting with confidence. Pick suits with sober, dark colors; suits made from linen are more preferred than cotton. Do not go with ties with garish patterns as they might distract interviewers.

Chapter 6: The Ballet, the Theater Night, or the Opera

Watching a play or going to the Opera is quite a unique experience than other forms of events. Despite the emergence of numerous entertainment options, live theaters and ballets have maintained their popularity. Unlike a game night or movie night, outfits of the audience greatly set the mood for the theater or the opera.

For Eves

Wearing casual to the theater play, the ballet or the opera is completely acceptable; however, that doesn't mean that it's the best choice. You have paid decent bucks for the ticket, so why to lose the momentum when it comes to selecting the attire. You can choose to wear broke and dress. Cocktail outfits are also an ideal fit for the special occasion as they provide the desired charm; go with a tailored shirt or gorgeous suit along with matching heels. And if you feel the strong desire to go in jeans then ensure that it has a dark wash without any distressing or holes.

For attending the opera party, many like to dress up in their favorite or popular opera characters to stand out from the rest of the crowd. It also enhances the opera theme and attracts the desired attention.

For Adams

Such a special occasion like the ballet or theater calls for a gentleman feel from men. It is expected from men to give respect to the dress code for the occasion and exercise punctuality. It's time to be a true gentleman.

Wear a Gentleman's Attire

The best suggestion is to consult with the management at the time of making the reservation. They can provide you with better insights about the dress code. For instance, if the occasion is the opening night then it's the perfect time to wear a stunning tuxedo to impress everyone out there. If you want to go with a sporty look then give yourself a gentleman touch with a lovely dress or polo shirt along with chinos. Additionally, you can wear a necktie for the perfect finishing touch. If you want to be more creative with your outfit skills then a custom suit tailored to your numerous preferences won't go a miss either. Jeans and flip flops are strictly not advisable as it will ruin the gentlemen's spirit expected for the occasion. Also, unless specified by the management, you should also avoid wearing a jacket and tie.

Chapter 7: Make a First Good Impression on Your First Date

Irrespective of your gender, the desire to look out of the world on your first date is quite common. Everyone wishes to be loved for their physical attributes as well as finer innate qualities, and wearing a gorgeous outfit takes them one step closer to be admired for these qualities.

For Eves

Fashion experts advice on selecting an outfit that can reflect your true personality as the first date is about being your true self; it's not a good time to take risks and do new experiments. Instead of going for the most spectacular outfit, chose the one that you feel great in it. Focus on being comfortable in your outfit as it will assist you in focusing more on your date partner. If you already have a pair of pants or an outfit of your favorite color that has showered you with a lot of compliments, then it's an ideal outfit for your first date. For instance, a feminine and colorful outfit such as a wrap dress that leaves something to your partner's imagination is the best choice to go with. Avoid outfits that are short or too tight; also, it's not suggested to try out multiples trends for just one evening or night. You don't want to spend your time on adjusting the outfit after every five minutes, so avoid wearing outfits that are too tight or too loose. Similarly, low-cut tops are also not suggested for special occasions such as a date.

The time is right to accentuate one's best assets. In order to focus attention on your face, go with pleasing dangly earrings or a fitted turtleneck. Similarly, outfits such as a wrap dress or V-neck beautifully and subtly highlights your busts. If your best asset is your waist then wear a spectacular belt; if it's your legs then go with skinny pants, dress, a short skirt or dress. If you feel that your top is too blousy then avoid wearing loose-fitting outfits as you can balance it out with a fitted bottom.

For Adams

Men preparing for their first date want their lady to take them seriously as the occasion can lead to something serious or a lifetime commitment. So be it a dinner date or casual one, picking the perfect outfit becomes an absolute requirement.

Casual Dates

Casual dates that are outdoors, call for more relaxed outfits, but without being sloppy. If the date includes any kind of sporting activity then pick an outfit that isn't dated or tattered. Avoid wearing work clothes or simple blue jeans as it might look like you haven't put any efforts in selecting the outfit.

Jeans that are dark-washed in deep indigo or black shade create a nice balance and they also go nicely with a dress shirt or collared shirt with short sleeves.

Dinners Dates

Wearing a stylish jacket is an ideal choice for dinner dates, especially planned in urban locations. One can also wear a matching suit, but if you are not comfortable with it then pick a blazer jacket matching with your skin complexion; blazer jackets are ideal for daytime dates and one can also replace it with flattering sporty jackets. Such jackets will provide you with the true masculine look.

Chapter 8: Shine Brightly at a Festive/Occasional Party

For Eves

The occasional, social, or festive party is the perfect occasion to dress up in a spectacular outfit to sparkle yourself. Whether you prefer glamorous glitter or subtle shine, it's time to give yourself a perfect party look.

Festive parties are great occasions to wear playful cocktail outfits. You can pick from numerous options from a print or bold colored dress to slinky tops along with dressy slacks. Also, a black dress with additional glittery items, such as chandelier earrings, or a fancy clutch is an apt choice. In case a festive party has a specified theme, care should be taken not to overdo it. You can go with large loop earrings and a stunning top. Following are two popular and trendy choices for the festive occasions.

The Cute Combination of Peplum-and-Pants
The cute combination delivers understated, sophisticated, and chic look. In case you feel the need to add more glamor then there are always jewelry and metallic sandals for that.

The Classic Sweater and Pants

This classic combo is not only high in style, but it is also high in comfort level. If the occasion is more formal then wear stylish pants along with a camisole or sheer black blouse. The sweater also goes perfectly with jeans.

For Adams

Holiday parties demand a different treatment and special attention from men and women as compared to other occasions. It's different in many ways from dressing up for the theater, a wedding or a cocktail party.

Social Festive Parties

One of the best options for social parties is a lovely pair of jeans, unwashed dark rinsed denim or raw one; it might look a little dressier, but it fits in nicely with the environment. Also, one can opt for a clean shirt with a deep burgundy, navy, black or white shade. Also, tux jackets are not a bad choice; a black tuxedo jacket looks cool and fashionable on such occasions.

Casual Holiday Parties

Casual festive parties are the occasions that give liberty to loosen up a bit. Dress up in style with chinos or jeans along with a casual sweater or shirt instead of a sports coat.

Chapter 9: Dress Up Appropriately for a Wake or Funeral

A wake or funeral is probably the most delicate social affair that demands being respectful to its dress code. In a wake or funeral, the focus should be more on showing respect to the deceased and less on fashion.

For Eves

One doesn't need to always dress in black for sad occasions; your outfit should be respectful for such occasions. The ideal outfit should be a toned-down one such as forest green, brown, or navy shade; dresses made from lightweight wool and pantsuits are ideal ones. Discreet and dark patterns are acceptable choices such as stud earrings and pearls. Common outfit choices include pant suits, skirt suits, pant and top with long sleeves, skirt, and blouse, & skirt and sweater.

Useful Dress up Tips:
- Go with dark suits or dresses
- Always cover your shoulders
- Dresses and skirts must be long enough to cover knees
- Avoid bright shaded dresses

- Dresses that are overly revealing are should be strictly avoided.

For Adams

Suits

If you wish to go in suits, then dark shades are a must. Also a dark navy or gray colored suit is an apt choice. If you do not feel comfortable wearing a suit then you can go with dark dress pants along with a sophisticated shirt and tie.

If a funeral is taking place inside a church then it is advisable to keep your jacket on. If a funeral is taking place outside, in a warm weather then you can take off your jacket. Sneakers, jeans, t-shirts etc. are completely off the table as casuals are not an appropriate dress code for most funerals unless informed by family members.

Shirt/Tie

Either a black or white shirt is an acceptable choice of wear. You can go conservative with respect to neckwear. Pick simple and solid patterns only and avoid wearing anything bright or of loud patterns.

Conclusion

Pick any occasion we have covered in the book, one can't pick one choice that is absolutely right or wrong. The suitability of your outfit is based on end number of factors such as the type of occasion, skin tone, weather conditions, fabric type, body curves and other physical attributes. Do not leave the decision the pick the perfect outfit to the last moment as it is only going to increase your stress level.

Keep numerous occasions, covered in this book, in mind and consider a range of styles to pick from. Understand what is the ideal dress code for different occasions and dress up accordingly to look fashionable, smart and most importantly at your best!